BATTLE AGAINST LEPROSY

THE STORY OF STANLEY BROWNE

Nancy Martin

RELIGIOUS AND MORAL EDUCATION PRESS
An Imprint of Pergamon Press

Religious and Moral Education Press
Hennock Road, Exeter EX2 8RP
An Imprint of Pergamon Press

Pergamon Press Ltd
Headington Hill Hall, Oxford OX3 0BW

Pergamon Press Inc.
Maxwell House, Fairview Park, Elmsford, New York 10523

Pergamon Press Canada Ltd
Suite 104, 150 Consumers Road, Willowdale, Ontario M2J 1P9

Pergamon Press (Australia) Pty Ltd
P.O. Box 544, Potts Point, N.S.W. 2011

Pergamon Press GmbH
Hammerweg 6, D-6242 Kronberg, Federal Republic of Germany

Photographs are reproduced by kind permission of Dr Stanley Browne.

First published 1985

Printed in Great Britain by A. Wheaton & Co. Ltd, Hennock Road, Exeter

ISBN 0 08-031750-2 non net
ISBN 0 08-031751-0 net

BATTLE AGAINST LEPROSY

The Story of Stanley Browne

From the time Stanley Browne was five he had wanted to be a missionary.

He was not a particularly good boy, nor was he especially brave like the missionaries he read about and those who came to speak at church and Sunday school. Very determined and strong-willed, he could be mischievous and cheeky at times, too. In fact, he was an ordinary, healthy boy, good at sports and popular with the other boys.

His two young sisters thought the world of him, though if he corrected their mistakes too often they would say, a little peevishly, "Oh, Stanley's *always* right". But he was the brother who played with them and took them on outings, carrying them on his shoulders when they were tired.

Stanley's parents were happy and hard-working, and their five children were expected to work hard too. Their mother taught them all to cook, and gave each of them a job to do in the house. She insisted that they did their homework straight after tea.

Stanley (far left) and the Browne family, 1919

Sundays were active days in the Browne family. Stanley's father was secretary of Drummond Road Baptist Church in Bermondsey, south-east London. As soon as they were old enough, the children walked to church with their parents on Sunday mornings. Their mother had been secretary of the Sunday school where Stanley and his elder brother, Frank, were among the eight hundred scholars on Sunday afternoons.

Like his grandmother, who lived with them, Stanley had

a very good memory, but it was not until he left primary school and went to Brockley Central School that he settled down to study. There he found that, if he worked hard enough, he could succeed. He started to come top in most subjects and later became head boy. His headmaster was proud of him.

Stanley had high hopes for his future. He wanted to stay at school until he was sixteen and go on to university. But suddenly his hopes and plans were shattered. His father was cycling home from work when he was knocked down by a steam traction-engine. His leg was crushed and for five months he was in hospital and the family had to exist on half pay. Stanley had to leave school and go to work. He got a job in Bermondsey Town Hall as a clerk.

This was a bitter blow for the boy but he was still determined to get to university. On four nights a week he studied at evening classes. It was tough going. Every morning he got up at six to read his Bible, spend time in prayer, and do his homework before going to work.

On Saturday afternoons Stanley and his brother Frank cycled into the country with a group of young people, stopping on village greens to conduct services. Stanley was often the preacher.

One day the Sunday-school superintendent asked him to take on a class of really tough boys.

"Three teachers have tried to tackle them," he told Stanley, "but they've all given up. I'd like you to see what you can do with them."

Stanley accepted the challenge. More than fifty years later one of his former pupils remembered those times:

"We really were a tough and disorderly crowd, but Stanley had a remarkable effect on us. We all adored him and would do anything for him. He knew how to put over a good yarn and he took us to camp. When it was time to leave Sunday school some drifted away, but the rest of us stayed on."

For four years Stanley continued studying at evening classes. Then the London County Council offered some of their brightest students a chance to win a scholarship to a university of their choice. To his surprise and delight Stanley was invited to County Hall for an interview.

But once again tragedy struck the Browne family. Only a few days before the interview, Stanley's mother, who had always been very healthy, became seriously ill and was taken to hospital for an operation. Stanley went to see her on his way to County Hall. She died before he left the hospital.

Medical training

A few months later Stanley was offered a two-year scholarship at King's College in London. At first he thought he ought to stay at work and help keep the home going, but the rest of the family urged him to accept the offer, and that settled it.

When he was quite young he had gained a certificate in first aid. That, and seeing the care the doctors had given his parents in hospital, had made him think about becoming a *medical* missionary. During his two years at King's everything seemed to be pointing him in that direction, and he applied for an extension of his grant so that he could take the full medical course.

The London County Council had been watching his progress. This boy was winning his way by sheer hard work and merit. He deserved to be encouraged and they granted the extension.

Now Stanley had a definite goal. "I am determined to devote my life to the relief of suffering, and to the causes of disease, and to find a cure," he said to a friend. "With God's help I'll do it."

His friends knew that he meant it. They knew that he wanted to go to the Belgian Congo (now Zaire), where medical missionaries from the Baptist Missionary Society were working.

The extra years of training were busy and tough. When it was time to do his practical work in medicine, he aimed for the top. He secured the post of house physician to the senior physician, then became house surgeon to the senior surgeon at King's. These jobs gave him just the experience he needed. Sometimes the senior surgeon would say to him, "You do this, Browne. You may meet with something like it in Africa."

Everyone was helping him towards his goal and Stanley was determined to go to Africa with the highest possible medical qualifications. That was why, when he had completed his training at King's, he went to Antwerp, in Belgium, to take a course in tropical diseases.

In 1936 he was ready to travel to Africa as a Baptist missionary doctor.

Africa at last

Stanley left the ocean liner at the busy port at Matadi, on the estuary of the Congo river, and boarded the train to Leopoldville (now Kinshasa), capital of the Belgian Congo.

As the train made its way through deep gorges and over mountains, Stanley tried to imagine what the journey had been like before the railway line opened in 1898. In the late nineteenth century, missionaries had had to travel on foot, with Africans carrying the loads. It was a long, hard trek across rough terrain. At that time the region was ruled by King Leopold II of Belgium, who had gained control of the country in 1885 and named it the Congo Free State, or the Independent State of the Congo. The Europeans who settled there had exploited the mineral wealth and the forests, and often treated the inhabitants unfairly. However, after the Belgian Government took over the country in 1908, when it was renamed the Belgian Congo, conditions began to improve.

Stanley remembered that it was the explorer Henry Morton Stanley who, in a remarkable adventure, had sailed the full length of the Congo river and opened up the lower and upper reaches of the river for trade. The Congo drains the massive Congo Basin and is the largest river in Africa, but ocean-going vessels can travel only about 140 kilometres inland from the mouth of the river, as far as Matadi. Rapids and waterfalls at the western rim of the Congo Basin prevent them reaching the interior.

It was with a feeling of adventure that Stanley boarded the plane at Leopoldville. In 1936 it was not usual for missionaries to travel by air, and this was Stanley's first flight. Soon they were flying over the vast forest. Stanley could just make out some villages near the river banks, but apart from a few wisps of smoke rising from the forest, there was little sign of habitation. From the air, the palm trees looked like ferns and the river a mere trickle.

A few minutes before the plane touched down at the airport at Stanleyville (now Kisangani), Stanley had his first glimpse of the mission station at Yakusu. About twenty kilometres up river he could see the corrugated iron roofs of the missionaries' bungalows next to the two-storey hospital.

Raymond Holmes, the doctor with whom Stanley was to share the work in an area the size of Wales, was on the tarmac waiting to greet him. A small African boy stood near by.

"This is Lofanga, your houseboy," Holmes explained. "He's one of our schoolboys. He asked if he could work for you now that Dr Chesterman has gone to England."

Stanley held out his hand and Lofanga seized it with a wide grin; it was the beginning of a long friendship between the two.

At the river bank stood a dozen powerfully built Africans, each holding a paddle nearly four metres long. In the water was a long canoe hewn out of a tree trunk. Stanley lowered himself carefully into the canoe, followed by Lofanga and Holmes. The twelve men took up their positions, pushed their paddles into the water and they were off, the crew singing their welcome to Stanley as they paddled.

At the villages they passed, groups of people stood on the bank to greet them, while the drum beat out the message to the next village: "The white doctor is coming". Before they reached Yakusu the huge mission drum could be heard sounding out its welcome.

Stanley was astonished by the scene that greeted him. A thousand schoolchildren lined the bank, singing. Mr and Mrs Millman, the senior missionaries, who had walked that long, wearisome journey to Leopoldville nearly forty years before, welcomed him warmly. Beside them stood a tall, slim African, who was introduced as Lititiyo. Stanley had heard his story but it was difficult to believe that he had been a cannibal when Mr Millman first met him, in a riverside village. Lititiyo was now a Christian pastor and had charge of Christian congregations in sixty river and forest villages.

Missionaries, nurses and medical students added their welcome when Stanley mounted the jetty steps. He felt relaxed and happy as he made his way to the bungalow he was to share with Raymond Holmes.

In charge of the hospital

The Millmans had invited Stanley and Raymond Holmes to dinner that night. It was a clear, bright evening. As Stanley walked along the river bank to the Millmans' house he could see flashes of lightning in the distance and fireflies, like tiny flickering lights, in the lower branches of the trees. All around he could hear the clicking of crickets and the whizzing of tiny insects, occasionally interrupted by frogs croaking on the beach.

It was not so pleasant coping with the flies at dinner. They seemed to be everywhere, drowning in the water glasses, landing in the soup and flying on to Stanley's fork as he put it to his mouth. He was doing his best to overcome the fly problem when a boy brought a note for Dr Holmes. It was an urgent request for him to go down-river to visit a sick man.

"That leaves Stanley in charge of the hospital," said Mrs Millman. "We usually give newcomers a day or two to settle in."

"Well, tomorrow's Sunday, when we only do routine work," Dr Holmes reminded her, "unless there are emergencies, of course. I'm sure Sister Moyles will manage, and Lotoba will be there." He turned to Stanley. "Lotoba is our chief medical auxiliary. He's very capable."

Stanley did not have a restful night. The air was hot and sticky, rats were having fun rolling palm nuts in the roof, and the noisy chorus of owls, hyenas, jackals and crickets outside the bedroom window disturbed his sleep.

The ward was crowded when Stanley was called there early next morning. There were people everywhere: on the floor, beside the beds and even under them. As many as three people were sharing some of the beds. He made his way to a room where a pregnant girl was screaming. Three women, besides the nurse, were trying to comfort her.

"Can't you get some of these people out of here?" he asked Sister Moyles. He could hardly hear himself speak.

"No, it's better they stay. Our patients feel safer if their relatives are with them. Besides, they help look after them and cook their food."

So that was the reason for the overcrowded wards. Yakusu was going to be quite a change from the calm, clinical atmosphere of the English hospitals Stanley was used to.

On that first day in the hospital he saw something of the malnutrition, diseases, ignorance and superstitious fears of people who lived far from Yakusu. Some had walked or been carried by relatives long distances through the forest to reach the hospital. Some of the patients were screaming, not from pain, but because they had found chicken bones and blood scattered outside their huts. They were sure they had been bewitched and were going to die. When they were frightened or angry these people could become very aggressive.

At first Stanley worked mainly in the hospital. He became accustomed to starting the day with the sound of the drum at half past five. By six o'clock he was taking the roll-call of the medical auxiliaries. Then there was a brief period of worship before patients' bulk rations for the day were distributed. These included dried fish, plantain, rice, palm oil and sometimes monkey-meat if any had been brought in by the hospital hunter. Stanley began to understand how useful it was to have patients' relatives around to cook their food. A short ward-round was followed by breakfast, unless there were emergencies to be dealt with. For breakfast there was pawpaw (a tropical fruit rather like a melon), porridge and occasionally eggs.

During the rest of the morning Stanley examined patients and performed operations. Sister Moyles was

Stanley holding twin babies born at Yakusu hospital

always there to assist, as were the medical auxiliaries. He had little time to learn Lokele, the local language, and was thankful for his knowledge of French, which his assistants understood and translated for him.

There were patients with a wide variety of diseases, the most common being yaws, tuberculosis, malaria, river blindness and leprosy. Some patients had been mauled or bitten by animals and there were children with stomachs distended by malnutrition.

One other important task that soon became one of Stanley's most interesting and rewarding duties was teaching medical auxiliaries about simple medicine and hygiene. These young Africans helped in the hospital in the mornings and attended classes in the afternoons. As children they had been to the village school and had then spent three years in the Central Mission School. After five years' study they would sit the state medical auxiliary examination, taking charge of isolated dispensaries during their final two years of training.

Stanley often had his evening meal alone, with Lofanga waiting on him. The small boy was always at his side, ready to translate and help him learn Lokele. In return, Stanley helped Lofanga with his French. In the evenings he wrote reports, did the hospital accounts and dealt with correspondence. At half past nine the electric generator was turned off, but Stanley often continued to work by the light of a hurricane-lamp.

Into the forest

Holmes returned from a journey with the news that twenty-three cases of sleeping sickness had been reported in the Topoki forest.

"If it spreads we shall soon have hundreds of cases on our hands," he told Stanley. "Will you go and investigate?"

Stanley was eager to go. His predecessor, Dr Clement Chesterman, had been the first to use a very active medicine to cure this tropical killer disease, but there were many villages in the Topoki forest where no white doctor had ever been.

Bicycles were the only means of transport through the forest at that time. Lotoba and Esau, their cook, rode behind Stanley and Lofanga rode pillion on Stanley's bike. They often had to dismount and carry their bikes over fallen trees and across rickety bridges. It was a relief when they reached the first village and found that the teacher evangelist had gathered the villagers together, ready for treatment, outside the rest-house he had prepared for the visitors.

Stanley was very impressed by the dedication of the teacher evangelists he met. After their training, these men went to live in remote areas, where they ran small schools single-handed and held religious services. The villages they

Pastor Lititiyo (seated) and a group of teacher evangelists

worked in tended to be lonely, dismal places, and the villagers, whose lives were a constant struggle against infection and disease, were superstitious and uneducated.

In each village Stanley put on his white coat, set up his folding table and arranged his microscope while a noisy crowd gathered round him. The villagers were sometimes afraid that he was going to inject them with poison, but seeing him put the needle in his own arm reassured them.

In one village a witch-doctor came forward. He wore an enormous head-dress of parrot's feathers, and a leopard-skin girdle. He seemed so curious that Stanley invited him to look through the microscope. When he saw the many tiny "worms" in a drop of his own blood, he could not believe his eyes!

Besides giving injections against sleeping sickness, Stanley treated people with tropical ulcers, yaws and malaria. This work was dirty and tiring, but it was what he had come to Africa to do, and he was happy to do it.

The squalor and disease in these villages bore no comparison to what he came across on a later journey, however. Although he had found a lot of cases of leprosy, he had not yet seen anyone suffering from the late stages of the most severe form of leprosy, known as lepromatous leprosy. There was no known treatment for this horribly disfiguring disease, nor had any vaccine to prevent it been discovered. Wherever Stanley went he asked about these advanced cases, but no one would admit to having any in their village. The village chiefs always told him, "There are none like that here", but Stanley knew there must be many such sufferers.

Then, one day, he saw them. Quite unexpectedly he came across a clearing cut out of the forest. As a doctor, he was accustomed to unpleasant sights, but now he stood dismayed, shocked and helpless.

They came crawling out of their huts and held out their ulcerated stumps of hands. With their paralysed and deformed limbs and ravaged faces, they were the most pathetic people he had ever seen. The stench from their decaying bodies was nauseating. The desperate expression in their eyes haunted him. Aware that others shrank from them, they showed despair mingled with shame.

Stanley was overwhelmed. He knew there were millions of people like these all over the world. He had never imagined anything quite so terrible. He did not shrink away but promised there and then not only to do what he could to help them, but to try to prevent others from becoming like them.

This incident was the beginning of Stanley's lifelong commitment to the prevention and cure of leprosy, a commitment that was to have far-reaching results.

On future journeys he set himself the task of learning to recognise early signs of leprosy in the patients he examined.

His friendly approach enlisted the help of chiefs, and even some of the witch-doctors. These men could detect the tell-tale patches of early leprosy. They would point out a shiny patch on a patient's skin which Stanley would not otherwise have recognised.

"See the colour of it," they would say. "And there's only a little sweat on this one." Then they would murmur, "That's the mother of the bad leprosy."

Stanley and his helpers moved from village to village and invited all the people to come and be examined. With the help of his medical auxiliaries, he observed and recorded results and reported them to the authorities.

"This must be the highest rate of leprosy in the whole world," they said, in astonishment. Stanley had discovered the facts and they knew his records were accurate. But even Stanley could not know how many more such sufferers were hidden in the forest.

Counting the cost

It was in the spring of 1940, while Stanley was on leave in England after his first term of service in Africa, that he met Mali Williamson and fell in love with her. She was the daughter of the Foreign Secretary of the Baptist Missionary Society and had been born in China when her parents were missionaries there. Before Stanley returned to Africa they were engaged. Mali agreed to follow him as soon as he had a home ready for her.

Meantime there was plenty to keep Stanley occupied. Although he felt terribly lonely on some of his journeys, he was doing the work God wanted him to do and he would not have changed places with the most eminent doctor in Harley Street.

When Mali did arrive she took a full share of the work.

While Stanley was at the hospital at Yakusu she either taught in the school, helped the medical auxiliaries with some of their subjects, or took charge in the dispensary, checking and dispensing drugs. She went with him on his journeys, visited the women in their homes and encouraged them to bring their children to the doctor.

In each village Stanley and Mali visited they held a service. Stanley talked to the villagers about God's love and promised to help them.

When Mali was expecting their first child they had to decide whether it was right for her to continue making these journeys to the forest villages. They prayed for guidance, as they always did when they weren't sure what to do. In the end they decided that, because she was doing God's work, Mali was right to take the risk. In due course, a healthy boy was born. They named him Derek.

Stanley, Mali and Derek on a journey through the forest, 1943

When Derek was nearly four years old, they had to choose between leaving him in England or giving up their work to stay there with him. In those days it was a mission rule that European children should not be brought up in the Congo. It was felt that all the African fevers and diseases made it too dangerous for them. So, while Stanley and Mali were on leave in England in 1945, they arranged for Derek to go to a boarding-school and be looked after by Mali's parents during the holidays. It was the greatest sacrifice of their lives.

However, the mission rule had been relaxed by the time their next two children, Alastair and Christopher, were born. The boys were allowed to stay with their parents in Africa until they were seven years old.

With Alastair, Christopher and some medical auxiliaries

The new drug

Until the 1950s, most people thought that, to control leprosy, patients should be kept in special hospitals. Having become aware of the extent of the disease, the Government was prepared to build a leprosarium (leprosy hospital) at Yalisombo, on the south bank of the river, opposite Yakusu.

Work went ahead quickly, but when the hospital was ready it was difficult to persuade patients to come.

"If you can't cure us we might as well stay in our villages and die there," they said.

Those who did come to Yalisombo said that the food was not good enough and there was not enough of it. Stanley spoke to the Belgian administrator and he promised to arrange for more and better food to be supplied.

For a time all went well but there was still no cure for leprosy and the injections were painful. Once more the patients returned to their villages.

There was plenty to discourage those who were trying to control this disease but they worked hopefully for the day when things would improve.

Then something happened which made everyone very sad. Dickie, a medical auxiliary who was working at a distant dispensary, thought he had leprosy. Stanley made a number of tests, hoping Dickie was mistaken, but he really did have leprosy. What was even worse, he had the bad kind, lepromatous leprosy. That this should happen to Dickie was a great blow to them all. Dickie was one of the most intelligent and reliable of the medical auxiliaries.

Dickie immediately moved into the leprosarium for treatment, although he knew his case was hopeless. All Stanley could do was give him medicines and see that he took them regularly.

Then an American leprosy mission sent Stanley a new

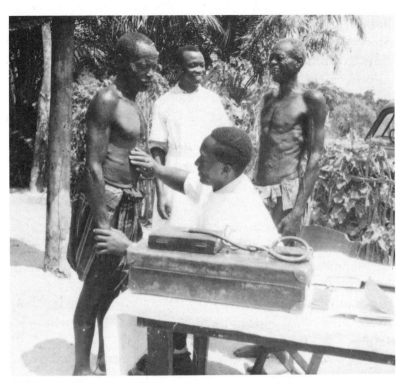

Dickie examining a leprosy patient

drug which had proved successful in curing leprosy in the United States. Stanley was asked to try it out. The American mission could not find out whether the drug would work in Africa unless patients were willing to try it. A volunteer was needed.

On his next visit to the leprosarium Stanley told the patients about the new medicine, and how it had cured leprosy patients in America. He did not hide the fact that the drug tended to have unpleasant side-effects, such as skin rashes, vomiting and diarrhoea. Then he asked anyone who was willing to take the risk to hold up their hand. Only one hand went up. It was Dickie's.

A long period of treatment began. Sometimes there was

hope and then some of the side-effects would appear.
Stanley and Dickie persevered, adjusting the dose from
time to time. At last Dickie began to show signs of
improvement. New hope was born. If someone with the
worst form of leprosy could get better there was hope for
all. As the treatment continued so did the hope of a
complete cure.

It came. The new medicine had arrived just in time for
Dickie. He was cured, and the cure proved permanent.

Opportunities unlimited

Now there was no difficulty in getting patients to come to
the leprosarium. More and more houses were built as
patients arrived from far and near until more than a
thousand patients were living at Yalisombo and thousands
more were being treated in the district dispensaries.
Patients in the early stages of leprosy could definitely be
cured by the new drugs, which were known as sulphones.

There were many visitors too. The news of what was
happening at Yalisombo was spreading, not only in the
Congo, but in other countries. Many came great distances
to see the results for themselves. No visitor was more
welcome than Dr Robert Cochrane, a world authority on
leprosy. What he saw impressed him enormously. In his
report to America he wrote that the laboratory and
dispensary buildings were first class and so was the work
being done by the doctor in charge. He added that the
records were the best he had seen and the clinical material
invaluable.

To Stanley he said, "Leprosy is a world-wide problem.
Research workers all over the world ought to be taught
what you know." He urged Stanley to concentrate on
leprosy.

This was an exciting and attractive idea, but Stanley had many other problems on his mind. He was concerned about people suffering from river blindness. This is a disease transmitted by the low-flying black-fly, which injects tiny parasites under the skin. It had always been around in the Congo but now these flies were multiplying, and the disease was spreading rapidly.

Stanley explained to his medical auxiliaries how the tiny, thread-like worms got under the skin. They caused intense irritation as they worked their way upwards until they reached the eyes, when they blinded or even killed their victims.

To stop the increase of the black-fly, they would first have to find its breeding-grounds. This meant looking for the larvae of the black-fly. Stanley had been told that they would find the larvae clinging to crabs in the fastest-flowing streams. He and his helpers spent weeks cutting paths through the forest to out-of-the-way streams. They examined thousands of crabs, without success. At last, however, Stanley turned over a crab that had dozens of larvae on it. He had found a stream where the black-fly bred. Redoubling their efforts, Stanley and the auxiliaries found several more streams.

Joyfully they set about disinfecting the streams. That done, they knew they were on the way to eliminating another tropical disease. What a mission!

By the time Stanley and Mali were due to go on their next leave, not only had river blindness been eliminated, but 2092 people had been cured of leprosy. Many had become Christians while at the mission and had returned to their villages to pass on the message.

One was Alieti, a cheerful little girl who had come to the mission hospital with leprosy. There was no school in her village and she could neither read nor write when she

Stanley and Mali at Yalisombo leprosarium

arrived, but she attended the mission school and was an intelligent pupil. She used to watch Stanley working in the clinic. When the patches on her skin had cleared up she was discharged from hospital and it was some months before Stanley saw her again.

When they visited her village, Stanley and his wife were greeted by a choir of boys and girls, conducted by Alieti, standing outside a new school. Alieti explained that when she came back from hospital she had asked some of the men to build a school of mud and thatch, with three class-rooms. She had persuaded three men who could read and write to become teachers. Alieti herself was the headmistress, although she was only twelve years old.

"When I was in hospital," she said, "didn't I learn to read and write? And didn't I learn about Jesus and decide to follow him? Now I am sharing with the boys and girls in my village the things I learned in hospital."

Then she took Stanley and Mali behind the school to another building. A group of men and women, as well as children, were standing outside.

"When I watched you in hospital," Alieti told Stanley, "I saw you look at patches on the skins of patients. I have collected here everybody with patches on their skin. I think some of them have leprosy." And they had.

The years of hard and unrewarding toil were beginning to bring their reward. Before Stanley and Mali went on leave, a thanksgiving service was held. It was known as the Grateful Samaritan Service. Three hundred people filled the church and there were three thousand more outside. They had come to watch as certificates of discharge were distributed to 102 patients who were returning to their villages, cured of leprosy.

There was joy on the faces of these people whom the missionaries had come to serve and who had become their friends. But Stanley and Mali sensed a feeling of sadness, too. Although their African friends were looking forward to their return, Stanley and Mali thought this was unlikely. Stanley was fifty years old. He had been at Yakusu for twenty-three years, and there were changes ahead. The African community was getting restless. They wanted independence, which was likely to be granted to them shortly. There was tension in the mission. Added to that, Stanley and Mali had missed seeing their boys grow up. Now they wanted to be with them more often. They had no plans for the future but they were prepared to wait and see where God led them.

Perhaps Stanley was remembering Dr Cochrane's advice that he should concentrate on leprosy in broader fields of service.

Mission world-wide

It was not long before Stanley and Mali were back in Africa. This time they went to Nigeria at the invitation of the Nigerian Government. In 1959 Stanley was appointed senior leprologist at the world-famous leprosarium in Uzuakoli. He was treating leprosy patients and sharing his knowledge of the control of leprosy with top researchers and governments all over the world, as Dr Cochrane had urged him to do.

The pattern of his and Mali's lives had changed. They now had a bigger and better house and, for the first time, a car. The boys were able to fly to Nigeria for their holidays, and their parents spent their annual leave in England.

During his second year in Nigeria Stanley had the opportunity to try out another new drug, referred to at that time by the code number B663 (it is now known as Lamprene or clofazimine). His patients in Uzuakoli were willing guinea-pigs. They trusted him as Dickie had done in Yalisombo. Stanley tried the drug on patients with lepromatous leprosy and they began to get better. The results were so encouraging that his medical assistants said they would ask to be given the drug if they ever caught leprosy.

In the early 1960s Stanley received two exciting invitations that would launch him on an international career.

First the World Health Organisation (W.H.O.) invited him to make a two-month tour of leprosy research centres in Africa, India and South-East Asia. During that time he lectured and helped with investigations in India, the Philippines, Malaysia and Hong Kong.

In September 1963 he chaired a working group at an International Leprosy Congress in Rio de Janeiro. This gave him an opportunity to talk to top researchers from all over the world, and to exert his influence on their governments. It was a tremendous challenge.

Stanley expected to remain in Nigeria for some time yet but his own country was calling him. Dr Cochrane was retiring from his position as Director of the Leprosy Study Centre in London, and also as Consultant Adviser to the Ministry of Health (now the D.H.S.S.), and Stanley was invited to succeed him. At the same time he was asked to become secretary and treasurer of the International Leprosy Association. These appointments would enable him to continue his travels while based in England.

He was now nearly sixty, an age when most people would be thinking of retiring, but Stanley felt that God was calling him into ever-broadening fields of service. After an exhausting tour of the United States on behalf of the American leprosy missions, he took up his new position in London.

During his time at Yakusu he had been awarded high

honours by the Belgian Government. In 1966 he was invested with the O.B.E. at Buckingham Palace. Later in the year he was again invited to the Palace, this time to lunch with the Queen.

Since 1966 Stanley has visited nearly seventy countries, advising governments and missions on leprosy and community health, helping thousands of leprosy sufferers and running seminars for leprosy workers. He has also written over five hundred scientific articles. No wonder he is known throughout the world as "Mister Leprosy".

Despite the efforts of Stanley Browne and others, it is estimated that there are still about fifteen million people suffering from leprosy. "We know enough but we are not doing enough to control the disease," says Stanley. His work goes on.

A visit to Nepal, 1979

BIOGRAPHICAL NOTES

8 December 1907   Stanley George Browne is born in New Cross, London

1923–27   Clerk, Town Clerk's Department, Deptford
1927–30   King's College, London
1930–33   King's College Hospital, London
1933–35   House physician, later house surgeon, King's College Hospital
1935–36   Institute of Tropical Medicine, Antwerp, Belgium
1936–58   Baptist medical missionary, Yakusu, Belgian Congo
1959–65   Director, Leprosy Research Unit, Uzuakoli, Nigeria
1966–80   Director, Leprosy Study Centre, London
1966–84   Secretary, International Leprosy Association
1966–81   Medical Consultant to The Leprosy Mission, the Hospital and Homes of St Giles, the Order of Charity, etc.
1968–73   Medical Secretary, LEPRA; 1984, Vice-President
1980–81   President, Baptist Union of Great Britain and Ireland
1984   Secretary, International Leprosy Congress, Delhi
1984   Chairman, Medical Committee, Conference for the World Mission of the British Council of Churches

Stanley Browne's numerous awards include:

1948   Chevalier, Ordre Royal du Lion
1958   Officer, Ordre de Léopold II
1965   Officer of the Order of the British Empire
1973   Commandeur, Ordre de Malte
1976   Companion of the Order of St Michael and St George
1980   Commandeur, Ordre de Léopold II

THINGS TO DO

A Test yourself

Here are some short questions. See if you can remember the answers from what you have read. Then write them down in a few words.

1 How did Stanley Browne's life change when his father had an accident?
2 When and why did Stanley decide to become a *medical missionary*?
3 How did he travel to Africa?
4 Why was Stanley made responsible for the hospital at Yakusu on his first night there?
5 What happened after Dickie was found to have leprosy?
6 How did village chiefs and witch-doctors help Stanley?
7 What did he do to prevent river blindness?

B Think through

These questions need longer answers. Think about them and then try to write two or three sentences in answer to each one. You may look up the story again to help you.

1 Stanley wanted to be a missionary when he was five. Why did he wait until he was twenty-eight before going to Africa?
2 Who were the medical auxiliaries, and what did they do?
3 When leprosy patients were cured a church service was held. Why was it called the Grateful Samaritan Service?
4 Describe the differences between a British hospital and the one at Yakusu.

C Talk about

Here are some questions for you to discuss together. Try to give reasons for what you say or think. Try to find out the different opinions which people have about each question.

1 Why do you think Stanley Browne wanted to work as a doctor in Africa instead of using his skills in England? Do you think he could have done just as well in this country?
2 When he was a student Stanley Browne kept a card on his desk that read "Perseverance leads to success". Do you agree with this saying?

3　Why do you think so many of Stanley Browne's patients became Christians and took the Christian message back to the people in their own villages?

D Find out

Choose one or two of the subjects below and find out all you can about them. History books, geography books and encyclopedias may be useful. Perhaps you can use reference books in your library to look up some of the names and places.

1　*Tropical diseases*
  (a) Describe the symptoms and treatment of one of the following: leprosy, malaria, yaws, sleeping sickness. How is the disease transmitted?
  (b) Find out what is being done to control leprosy by organisations such as LEPRA, the Leprosy Mission and the World Health Organisation (see p.29).
  (c) Write an account of the work of Father Damien, Paul Brand, Ida Scudder or Ruth Pfau (see p.29–30).

2　*Africa*
  (a) When was slavery stamped out in the Belgian Congo?
  (b) When did the Belgian Congo become the Democratic Republic of the Congo? When did the name change to the Republic of Zaire?
  (c) Draw a map of Zaire and mark on it Kinshasa, Lubumbashi, Kisangini, Kolwezi, Matadi and the Congo and Kasai rivers. Find out the names of the lakes on the eastern border of the country.
  (d) Write an account of Sir Henry Morton Stanley's travels in Africa, illustrated with a map.
  (e) Read about Albert Schweitzer (see p.29). What similarities can you see between his work and that of Stanley Browne? Compare the early life of these men.

3　*Baptists*
  (a) What are the principal beliefs of the Baptists?
  (b) Find out about one of the following: William Carey, Adoniram Judson, Martin Luther King.
  (c) When was the Baptist Missionary Society formed? What is its main role today?

USEFUL INFORMATION

Addresses

LEPRA (The British Leprosy
  Relief Association)
Suite 54
Manfield House
376 Strand
London WC2R 0LR.

The Leprosy Mission
50 Portland Place
London W1N 3DG.

American Leprosy Mission Inc.
One The Broadway
Elmwood Park
New Jersey 07407
U.S.A.

W.H.O. (World Health
  Organisation)
Avenue Appia
1211 Geneva 27
Switzerland.

Saint Francis Leprosy Guild
21 The Boltons
London SW10 9SU.

Zaire Embassy
26 Chesham Place
London SW1.

The Baptist Missionary Society
93–97 Gloucester Place
London WH1 4AA.

N.B. It is best if only one person in each class writes off for information. When writing to addresses in Britain, remember to enclose a stamped, addressed envelope for the reply. A postal order for at least 50p would also be helpful, if you want plenty of material.

More books to read
The Baptists, by John Wood (R.M.E.P.) (P).
Dr Ida, by Dorothy Clarke Wilson (Hodder & Stoughton), the
  story of Ida Scudder and the founding of Vellore (T).
Free at Last: Martin Luther King, by R.J. Owen (R.M.E.P.) (P).
The Great Doctor: Albert Schweitzer, by Nancy Martin (R.M.E.P.)
  (P).
The Healing Touch: Ruth Pfau, by Monica Wyatt (R.M.E.P.) (P).

Island of No Return: Father Damien, by Geoffrey Hanks (R.M.E.P.)
(P).

Mister Leprosy, by Phyllis Thompson (Hodder & Stoughton/The
Leprosy Mission) (T).

Paul Brand, by John Young (SCM Press) (T).

By Stanley Browne:

Leprosy in the Bible (Christian Medical Fellowship) (T).

Leprosy in England (available from St Giles Hospital, East
Hanningfield, near Chelmsford, Essex) (T).

Leprosy – New Hope and Continuing Challenge (The Leprosy
Mission) (T).

(T) = suitable for teachers and older pupils
(P) = suitable for younger pupils

Films

Leprosy (40 min), *Leprosy Can Be Cured* (15 min) and *Mariama* (22
min), all colour. Available from LEPRA or from Concord
Films Council Ltd, 201 Felixstowe Road, Ipswich, Suffolk
IP3 9BJ.

Lifted Hands (20 min), colour, by the Friends of Vellore.
Available from Concord Films Council.

Trained to Serve (22 min), colour, with speaker. Also on video.
Available from the Leprosy Mission.

Slide set

Journeys of Sir Henry Morton Stanley from 1871 to 1889. Available
from The Slide Centre, 143 Chatham Road, London SW11
6SR.

Other resources

Filmstrips, booklets, posters and other material about leprosy
can be obtained from LEPRA and the Leprosy Mission.